HUES OF HUMANITY

HUES OF HUMANITY

Carlin W. Allen

COPYRIGHT DISCLAIMER

The works presented in this book are based off of my own personal memories, told from my perspectivë, and I have tried to represent events as faithfully as possible. Some scenarios presented or described in this book are fictitious. Any similarity to actual persons, living or dead, is coincidental.

To request permissions, contact the publisher
at cwapoetry@pm.me
Instagram: @cwapoetry
Threads: @cwapoetry

Dedicated to the unread, unsung, unknown heroes of this increasingly small world-- those who 'fight the good fight' each day to make even one person's endless night just a little bit brighter.

Thank you.

The human mind is an amazing thing. From the pragmatic and logical to the spontaneous and creative, we are highly complex beings. The light of our souls is as rich, layered and varied as are the hues of the rainbow. This collection of poetry explores, from an emotional perspective, what it means to be human—as told through the subjective, but relatable lens of my own personal experiences.

AUTHOR'S BOOKS

Hues of Humanity: A Poetry Collection
Threads of Bohemia: Another Poetry Collection

TABLE OF CONTENTS

At the base of steep, daunting heights,
towering betwixt dark and light
scrutinize looming, eastern skies
For tomorrow's waxing rise
draws nigh, dawn's loving respite

SEASONS OF LIGHT

CHAPTER ONE: SPRING GREEN

"WISHING STARS"

Leisurely upon our bed we lie,
made of bubbles, wildflower petals, dreams.
The sounds of giggles and whispers suffuse,
carried by a soft breeze wafting downstream,
blowing dandelion clouds through the sky...

Without regard to place or time, carefree,
focused solely on laughter in our eyes--
somewhere in secret fields of varied hues,
like two spies with their eyes on the grand prize,
composing effervescent melodies...

For once, a mild sun orbits overhead,
as it traverses the long horizon.
Dreading the trip back home, away from you,
where years upon my face parch and wizen,
I decide to hold you longer instead...

Beneath those wishing stars, hidden from view,
dreaming under moonlight only we knew...

"WHEN EVEN THE RAIN STOPS FALLING"

There was a time when,
before worlds would end,
mankind's continued sins--
not lust, or greed, or gluttony,
neither hate, nor sickly jealousy,

Rather, pride, pretense, apathy
brought ruin, and drought, and expiry...
But by compassionate rains,
renewed were the dry, parched turves,
granting mercy undeserved.

"FEEL-GOOD JAUNT"

A sprightly breeze carries ancient strains
fervently hummed by forbears long since passed,
resonating with my ardent soul,
in sonic streams, infinitely vast,
undulating as they course through my veins.

Balmy sun rays unveil forgotten trails,
revealing meadows of vibrant tones,
with no agendas, no hidden goals,
as rhythmic ribbons pervade my bones,
grandly weaving anew time-honored tales.

"MAYBE THIS TIME"

The next semester had begun,
big city with a small-town feel
Much of the same, with no appeal--
endless tracks with nowhere to run...

Rolling hills were green, like sylvan dreams,
despite long years of dystopic fears,
frozen tears buried with mangled bears,
pale faces not seen since 'Temkin screamed.

But soon, all the dust from these broken dreams
settled in this kid of barely fifteen,
trapped in a mess of a man whose life theme
crashed with jagged dissonance...

Yet in that moment when
our eyes met once again,
I began to live, to breathe,
to think, to hope, to believe—

Everything will turn out completely fine...

Maybe this time.

"BEYOND THE DAWN"

Come sit with me a while, once more,
beneath the moonless onyx sky.
We can watch fire diamonds fly by,
on this night unlike any before.
Wondrous beauty like Phoenix plumes,
rare as her golden-scarlet tears,
crafted with care five hundred years.
Borne of blazing blossoms in bloom.

Dazzling like stars,
in your soul's eyes.

As we speak of times come and gone,
a gentle breeze blows through your hair.
I begin to think this is where
we would stay beyond the dawn,
watching the early morning rise
to electric sounds of drums, bass.

We'd slow dance in love's sweet embrace,
dreading when we would realize…

The end had come
to our magic night.

Often I'd peer across the sea,
thoughts on the one who stole my heart,
mulling o'er why we strayed apart.
Yet, here you are, in front of me,
so let us wind back Father Time,
kindling again the fire's light,
watching the Phoenix dance, take flight,
as the midnight sky she climbs.

Safe and free, somewhere
beyond the dawn.

CHAPTER TWO: SUMMER YELLOW

"DRUNK, ON LOVE"

You are my natural high.
Soaring, in your smile each day,
my heart melts,
like snow cones in a heatwave.

You are my soul's delight.
Drunk, on love as bubbly warm,
velvet smooth,
as cinnamon chai spritz, in free form.

You are my mind's cry.
Blown, by your explosive kisses,
snapping belts
upon fresh skin, with no misses.

You are my neon butterfly,
floating, bright as newlywed bride.
Pure as youth.
Beauty personified.

"SUBLIMATION OF FLIGHT"

We're here, visiting the valley,
a small tavern down the alley.
You're standing right across the bar,
surrounded by folks near and far.
My eyes are engrossed with your style.
I'm captivated by your smile.
Moonlight illumines your deep browns.
You glance. I quickly turn around.

Racing, my blood begins to flow.
My cheeks give off a telling glow.
Truly enamored by your laugh,
my heart's feeling less split in half.
Just as I mass ebbing courage,
I hear your name, an ill-timed page.
Possibilities wear and fray,
as you retreat and walk away...

Catching you on the edge of eye,
conversing with some other guy,
I watch our future dim and fade,
my only hand never to be played.
The deejay starts "Mr. Bright Side."
My self-doubt, I try to abide.
Defeated, I get up to leave,
no connection left to achieve...

Head hanging low, tail between thighs,
swiftly I impart my goodbyes.
Walking to the door, painted black,
I feel a soft touch on my back.
I turn towards you, simpering.
Dejection turns to newfound zing!
You slip your number in my fist.
Blushing, we part after long kiss...

Humming, I walk to the train,
nothing but romance on the brain.
I head home at slow, steady pace.
Warm, with a big smile on my face.

"FEAST OF TWO RIVERS"

Upon bygone, unfathomably battered shores,
softly hummed an unsung, melodic strain
conceived by unopened eyes sublime.
A sapphire-like cornflower sheened
'midst obscuring, fractured shells...

Serendipitously,
two short of two scores,
blessed with he, scaled
one for three,
he spied...

Me

"PRO CAROLO"

For Charles

Wafting gently like a midsummer's breeze,
whence on high chorus seraphic mercies,
without constraint, lucent love you endue,
whose ascent gifts luminary respite
warming frigid, snowy stone and spirit

Empathic dayspring flows to eventide,
ebbing therefrom, tender heart bona fide.
Each wave with undeserved kindness imbued,
ere returned anew to me, still tempered--
E'er cherished. E'er beloved. Nunc et semper.

"OUR SWEETEST MEMORY"

I woke up to baby paws to the face.
My ear received an unexpected wash,
as I scowled and turned the other way.
Mouths met clumsily over breakfast nosh,
and your giggly smile brightened my day…

On our way to work, we were stuck in line.
Every single road was jammed with rage.
But as we inched towards the on-ramp sign,
you said let's ditch the world, exit this cage.
And our devious smiles lightened that May…

We drove through the hills faster than the wind.
Finally alone, we let down our hair.
As we circled around the road's sharp bends,
our troubles flew down with exquisite flair.
And your carefree smile heightened our stay…

Beneath the summer stars we headed home,
my head on your shoulder, hands intertwined.
As I thought back on how far we had come,
you leaned and softly kissed these lips of mine.
Our enamored smiles enlightened our way…

At our door, you wanted to say something.
You held my hand and told how you love me.
As you placed on my finger a gold ring,
your words stuttered and stumbled, nervously.
But my unfrightened smile widened to say,

I'd give every day from today to
share one more day of our sweetest memory.

CHAPTER THREE: FALL BROWN

"MISCONCEIVED"

On the tenth month of the tenth year,
first row in a show of first times,
the stage light kissed us differently,
strumming uncharted paradigms,
acoustic strings, like puppeteers...

Though we must have gazed ten thousand stars,
connecting ten thousand lonely souls,
the way yours gazed back at me, gently,
sparked a keen fire I could not control,
when 'Satellites' projected my heart...

But when seasons erased those star-crossed skies,
December led to monochromic views,
and sickly snow angels fell fervently,
crashing beyond the frequency of you,
robbing the magicked light filling your eyes...

Though a million moments flickered and faded,
and waterfalls have long-since trickled and dried,
as these same stars gaze at me, attentively,
I sometimes wonder if that night, you too cried,
when misconceived projections were abraded...

By stark sands of unrequited reality.

"AS A ROSE GOES"

A rose can be only a rose,
whether fragrant, fair, and refined,
or thorny, putrid, and morose,
by name, by hue, or word defined,
a rose, is solely a rose...

A rose can see but as a rose,
not daffodil, basking in sun.
Neither lily, pure as fresh snow,
nor geranium, bright and fun.
A rose is, yet still, a rose...

A rose carefree is, again, rose.
When showered by autumn rains--
on remote shores, where tempo slows,
green in envy, with weathered veins--
a rose is, once more, a rose...

A rose can plea, only as rose.
Beneath cold skies, and sullen moon,
dreaming of one more to hold close,
hearts softly beating in tune,
a rose is, alas, a rose...

A rose for me, though, is a rose--
delicate like hummingbird wings,
nourished by tender hands enclosed--
rare and dear, as love enduring.
A rose is, at <u>least</u>, a rose!

A rose can be <u>more</u> than just rose--
sweet flower, and fervent promise;
heartfelt and honest poem in prose;
precious, special, like love's first kiss.
A rose is, seldom... 'just' a rose.

"WHEN LOVE IS DENIED"

Fifteen days have passed like fifteen long years.
Still sweeping up glass from our broken home,
and within each shard, grains of childlike fears.
Each one played, like cards in a hurtful game,

Where winners lose, and losers break...

Fifteen weeks went by like fifteen decades.
Tales of love denied circulate, then calm,
with 'tears and journey,' ended tales crusade,
yet on bended knees, slowly melting film,

Watching frayed frames bubble and bake...

Fifteen months were spent like fifteen centuries.
Seasons came and went, as skies stormed, then cleared.
Home's still vacant, cold— sterile, like bare trees.
We vowed to grow old, but you departed.

I'm still here, alone and awake...

Fifteen years squalled some fifteen thousand rains.
Fifteen more I'd give to hold you again...

"LABORS OF LOVE"

Fragile is the balanced life.
Even more so, divine abode,
built upon butterfly wings.

When fanciful folly fades,
rose-colored specs dull and grey,
none but dreams of tempered glass live on--

Forged in flames of undying resolve,
formed of humble truth...

Ere goes fleeting presence of mind
or compassionate hearth....

Seek out starry paths in loving silence,
not mortal cycles of lust, dissonant distrust...

For bitter, desiccated, and gritty
are fruits grown in ignis fatuus.

"COAHOMA, PART ONE"

Upon flaming, fleeting forested glade,
lay widowed cougar with her nascent son,
hemorrhaging lungs pierced by foreign blade.

As stifling smoke billowed through noxious air,
to her unnamed cub she whispered yon,
with stern, albeit evanescent glare.

She said thus, "Vm vlla, last of our tribes,
let not fiery rage blacken thy heart;
even dazzling suns set with shifting tides...

"May unyielding love light untrodden trail..."
spoke she, as sequoias splintered apart,
"Choose to live, and learn, to recount our tale...

"On moonless night, discern thy people's cries,
who dub thee, 'Coahoma, Heir of Red,'
lest timeless saga dims, decays, then dies..."

Closing insentient eyes 'bove breathless breast,
his silent, teary torrents where she bled,
the last brave left toward horizon's crest,

Winter ahead, rays of fall at his back...

CHAPTER FOUR: WINTER WHITE

"MEA ORATIO AETERNA (MY ETERNAL PRAYER)"

For Mary Kim, and all who loved her

Magnus omnium rerum Excogitatoris,
lassis animabus,
hac praeterita nocte,
et longas noctes recentis praeteritae
pacem et misericordiam faciat.

Lacrimae familiarum
defunctorum benedicantur
luce magni amoris Intentoris
ut pacem inveniant,
solamen et solamen.

Sicut dictum
est et creditum,
Fiat.

May the great Designer of all things, to weary souls, make this last night, and the long nights of the recent past, peace and mercy.

May the tears of the families of the deceased be blessed by the light of the great love of the Intender, that they may find peace, comfort and solace.

As it was said and believed, so be it.

"WHERE"

Where does one go, when each place is the same?
Which path to take, when none take solid form?
What refuge is there from despondent storms,
when a home lay engulfed in toxic shame?

What does one say, to those who never listen?
What words take page, for an audience of one?
What does a soul weigh, to those who've outdone
every endeavor, breakthrough, and ambition?

How bright is a star, in the light of seven suns?
How big is the loss, of vagrant souls no one knew?
Where can the delicate maidenhair fern take root,
in the concrete jungles, where it dries, imprisoned?

As you lie prone, wounded with broken wing,
and a darkened sky forming overhead,
listen to the common nightingale sing,
does not the Earth feel every tear it sheds?

Would not worlds weep without the love it brings?

Though tiny, ordinary and plain,
and difficult to see in night's cover,
its sullen song rings out like widespread rain
as it laments its departed lovers,
would not even passersby mourn its swain?

In the boundless, cosmic Infinity,
the expiry of but one falling star
dims and dulls its dreamy, nighttime beauty
fleetly passing moments each of we are,
whose worth can't be measured by minds unfree.

Only by the discerning hearts and eyes
of empathic souls and lonely lovers
may your sweeping radiance be surmised.
Thus, in crestfallen ears, I sweetly purr,
and gently take your weary hands, to rise.

"WORDS LEFT UNSAID"

An unexpected exchange
stirs long-forgotten sentiments,
as a soft breeze suddenly conveys
lost diamantine sediments
from profundities estranged.

Reveries turn to yearning,
as a spirit of you takes shape,
formed of memories hereto decayed,
adorning silver, fey-like drapes.
The hands of time stop turning.

By the crystalline lagoon,
once imbued with my falling tears,
our favorite tracks start to softly play.
We bolero for weeks, e'en years,
beneath light of the full moon,

My head rests upon your chest,
listening to your pristine heart.
Your peaceful, dreamlike eyes draw my gaze.
Lips draw close. You gently impart
the kiss of my lifelong quest.

As all the words left unsaid
undulate as emotive waves,
dissolving eons of lovelorn haze,
we perpetually embrace,
'til the dawn begins to spread.

As the sun slowly rises,
and overtakes your argent light,
cognizant of fading dreams, your shade,
I grasp the apparition tight,
until form compromises...

Still, I awake...

Gentle golden light creates
upon teary, early morn dew,
the warm sparkle your loving eyes made...
Upon my breast, a remnant of you,
as lonely winter abates...

Like the heart's ache.

"FOR WHOM"

For whom does one write,
on pages unseen?
For whom does one sing,
in a crowd of machines?

Or chuckle, or cry,
or bid fair goodbye--
a lost lover's pine--
rife with pungent lines...

Whether true, in jest,
unyielding unrest,
failing to digest...
this... *foul* salt of mine?

I've offered freely,
without clause or fee...
given, no receipt,
'til bare and supine...

Now, and long before,
I wonder once more,
whom it was all for...
'lone, 'woke, on caffeine.

"WITHOUT YOU"

Sometimes I find myself dreaming,
in withered fields, without you there.
Adrift.
When I feel your warmth at last,
the rolling hills blossom and green,
as dandelion feathers float midair.
Unveiled.
Like the final act in a magic show,
full of mystery, wonder, glee.
A lost tale on forgotten tome,
of you,
and I, carried on clouds of butterflies.

Sometimes I find myself screaming,
in a never-ending nightmare.
A rift.
Somewhere between our vibrant past,
and the deflated "could-have-beens,"
lost to black, wondering when, why and where.

I failed.
Sifting through every moment I know,
hoping that someday, I will see
a road to bring me back home
to you—
to just hold you, in better climes.

Sometimes I find myself seeming
like the world is too cruel to care.
A shrift.
As pointless as this distance vast.
But in truth, I know what this means,
and a world without you, I cannot bear.
I sailed,
to the ends and back. There's nowhere to go
as blissful, blithe and heavenly
as the carefree dreams where I'd roam,
with you,
enraptured by your gentle eyes.

Sometimes I find myself streaming.
Not watching, just thinking, I stare.
A gift.
Love, kisses and hugs at breakfast,
away from those nightmarish dreams–
being without you, middle of nowhere.
Exhale.
Your warm, bubbly laugh radiates, and flows,
filling with smiles, each cell in me.
Atop our mountain, in the bromes.
Just you,
and I, for all time.

PHASES OF NIGHT

CHAPTER FIVE: SUNSET MAGENTA

"NO MATTER THE PRICE"

Yet another sunset draws to a close.
You stand against the arch, in silhouette,
staring out at the coming storms ahead.
Bleeding into view, like life, in vignette,
nescient of your beauty in orange-rose...

Another year has swiftly come and gone.
You sit outside, beneath the light of stars,
searching for a way back home to the dead.
While halls echo sounds of laughter, guitars,
not seeing the great deck of friends you've drawn...

As the blackest nights begin their attacks,
and our world comes crashing down from above,
I won't let the darkness decay or spread
through the magnificence of our *real* love.
I'll fight each shade 'til you've found your way back—

Here, in those bright, beautiful amber eyes,
before your entire life passes us by...

No matter the cost. No matter the price.

"REVERIES AT DUSK"

The sun slips away, as dusk sets in,
eclipsing shadows where light had been.
Memories of an age passed softly shine,
as they swirl in the back of my mind--
long forgotten starlight from afar,
entombed, like fireflies in a jar,
then released into the dark night sky.
Questions, without answers, wonder why.
Arid sands of time flow slowly back,
bringing life to encompassing black...

Before me resides a cackling fire,
fed by passion, wonder and desire.
With windswept hair upon their faces,
twins of Gemini take their places.
Blowing tenderly, they weave their tale,
as the heart stone the twosome unveil,
casting it into the gleaming blaze.
Requiems for bygone love, one plays.

His ocarina between his hands,
inert silhouettes begin to dance...

A newborn rose, bare, in morning dew,
exhibiting its unforeseen hue.
Toward the sun, its endearment grows.
Prismatic rainbows begin to glow.
Unabated, it unwraps its core,
releasing fragrance never smelled before.
Wafting through the air by gentle breeze,
entrancing the nearby bumblebees.
Upon their bodies, its floral germs,
departing on no uncertain terms.

Task done, the sun retreats from above.
The rose left with unrequited love,
as the warm daylight begins to wane.
Frigidity spreads through its weak veins,
carried by winds which whistle and howl.
In the nighttime, they grumble and growl.
Forlorn in the storm, it starts to wilt,

Riddled with regret, suns without guilt.
Snuffed out in silence, its petals drop,
until heart, soul, feeling, lifeblood... stop.

The flames of antiquity subside,
as timeless sands give way to the tide.
The daydream the tuneful twins does rend--
fleeting fantasy, brought to its end.
Alone in the dark, I begin to brood,
about the seeming absence of good.
But then, the pale moon begins to rise,
and shine down where hope flickers and dies.
A familiar scent tickles my nose.
Hiding from my eyes—a shy, new rose.

"POSTMODERN RECONSTRUCTION"

Crimson softly glows behind ranges of grey and black.
A cool breeze staidly blows through smoky plumes.
Murders of homeless crows huddle atop distant stacks.
Sooty suits sweep with beaten, broken brooms,
as oceanic lashings inundate the last of ireful fires.

Cardinal capitols, housed by bulwark walls,
once proud, unshakably firm and resolute,
now crumbling and cracked, tumble and fall
from their burdensome, beleaguering buttes—
remnants of ruinous empires

Despotic canons forborne, paupers and princes alike,
indistinguishable, interchangeable, parallel in reposes.
Grayed men array plighted poppies on a pike,
lads and lasses soothed by maternal peach roses,
picked by beholden hands from brutal briars.

Resilient redwoods stretch their regal crowns,
silently soaking in dawn's first, homely rays—
respite hues of oranges and golden browns,
as reticence subsides to calls from Steller's jays,
perched up on high, on sympathetic spires.

"BE PROUD, STAND TALL"

You sit on the curb, on your own
pondering over times come and gone.
The fall from the top to bottom,
wondering where your doom came from.
Prismatic tears drop from your eyes.
You think of all the reasons why.
An unbearable angst sets in.
You push the needle to the vein...

Maybe if you were more a man,
or if you lived as per their plan.
If your nails were not painted black,
or you didn't run from that quack.
You shouldn't have worn that pink dress,
or tried to weigh a little less.
You slowly push the plunger through,
to forget what is wrong with you...

You deserved that bloody beating.
If only you had stopped breathing—
wouldn't be such an epic fail.
If you were stronger, not so frail.
Why can't you be the one they want,
instead of the queer one they taunt?
Eyes roll to the back of your head.
Perhaps all's better if you're dead...

You don't know, but I've been watching,
since the hour you started hatching.
Though you may feel loved by no one,
just know that you are not alone.
By their weak minds, be abashed not.
Let your saga thicken the plot.
Born unique, be proud and stand tall.
Break through this isolating wall.

You may feel unworthy of love,
but know you're a gift from above.
You merit a jovial life,
a caring man, a doting wife.
Triumph in feats, learn from mistakes.
Be referred to as a "snowflake."
Each made special, distinctively,
born exactly as meant to be.

"WHAT I COULD NEVER SAY"

At four years old, I was crossed by new gloves,
thrown in a mix, with no time to adjust,
wanting a hug, but given a blue truck...

At fourteen years, I was lost by your eyes,
a mere candle caught dreaming of your light,
completely oblivious it was mine...

At twenty-four, I was embossed by love—
not for the real, but for mind-blowing lust,
enchanted by gleams of recycled luck...

At thirty-four, I was tossed by your vice,
despite the real promises made that night,
drunk on oil, vinegar and cheapened wine...

At forty-four, I'm defrosting thereof,
learning to shed the shrewd veils of distrust,
to discern love's true light in the moonstruck.

CHAPTER SIX: EVENTIDE BLUE

"RULES"

Rules.
I laugh at your rules.
From homochromatic dotted lines,
drawn perfectly straight down my curved spine—

To 'actual' lines.

In hotel bars. At grand cafés,
formed by those who still wait on those acting with scripts—

Conscripts.

Written in the finest of prints.
Vague and small, and forcing squints.
Demanding of we fools, those
excessively, egregiously, exorbitantly extraordinary—

'Fees.'

As if anyone 'actually' had any money.
And for what, exactly?

Rules.
I chuckle at rules.
Conceived and born from a Cosmos without bounds,
but learning, and living, and dreaming and dying—

In a box,
lying deep underground.

And I keep asking myself, why?
What is it all for?

With such passion, and drive, even in prose,
to succeed, and be happy, and thrive with
everything needed in front of the nose,
why then, friend—

Dispassionately chore?

Over paper and deeds,
made of numbers and rules,
never hydrating,
feeding with soulful fuels...?

So...
why not break free?

Let go of the dots and the lines,
choosing colorful skeins only seen
by undaunted dreamers daring to dream
beyond boxes and boundaries.

Limitless.

In thought, in goodwill.
In good cheer, inner peace.
Living in love, and loving in life.

Unruled.

"WHILE YOU WERE ON VACATION"

While you were on vacation,
touring the sunny Shangri-Lan straths,
piercing dystopian dissonance
plagued the slummy streets.
As you devoured dignitaries' delicacies,
wrought by bloodied hands,
the wretched, the weary, rummaged
to quiet qualms of fleeting flesh.

You claim saintly saviorhood,
while cutting corpses of dissenting defectors,
soliciting subordinates, and sheepish slaves
as shields, should scrutiny surface.
Fluffing façades of sand and smoke,
the ilk of illusions of dogmatic devotion,
as poverty, pestilence and death ensue,
unsated, unyielding, ubiquitous.

You scroll and "like"
passed impotent implorations for healing help,
while promoting pretenses of philanthropy,
and empathy, albeit entropically.
As you burrow behind
contemptuous cloaks of misguided misogamy,
the destitute drink lethal libations,
forever foraging for laudation, for Lilliputian love.

So, spiel salacious stories of corporeal conquests,
eternal entitlement, sovereign sway.
Meanwhile, Madame Guillotine glistens,
sentiently sharpening her blade,
biding tempestuous torment
for certain, consuming change,
as you sanctimoniously shout,
stoking the furious flames of plebeian pique.

"WHO AM I?"

As a single drop in an endless sea,
one little star in heavens above me.
Like the dust settling on the Canyon floor,
an unquenched thirst always asking for more,
lost in the biting wind— a quiet sigh.
My quandary to you, "Who am I?"

In the multiverse, not even a blip.
From the barrel, a teeny, tiny sip.
Will you even remember my only note,
amongst all the timeless tunes the Greats wrote?
Through merciless monsoons, why even try?
I ask you once again, "Who am I?"

As festering air from hate begins to churn,
and Grandmother Cedar begins to burn,
the teary trails relentlessly repeat.
Pitiless patriots, incessant heat
obsessively obdurate as I rise,

defiantly whispering, "Who am I?"

I am the tale traversing time,
the unfettered eagle in its prime,
cutting through dystopian noise,
showing silence vehement voice—
clamorous claps through thunderous sky.
Armed with pride, I cry, "Who am I?!"

As you filch what none can own,
reaping harvests not yet sewn,
claiming privilege over the land,
bleeding Mother into sand,
reticent I'll no longer lie,
goading till I die, "Who am I?!!"

"IMPERFECTLY PERFECT"

Maybe I'm not as pretty as you.
Maybe I'm not as thin, it's true.
Maybe my skin is too swart,
or my eyes too far apart.
Perhaps less hair on my head.
But when you cut me, I bled.
You play that superficial game,
but overall, we're built the same.

So I never know how to start,
and on my sleeve, I wear my heart.
So I'm more awkward than some.
At least I dance to my own drum.
Though you stare at, and judge me,
through your façade I see—
just a little kid with a mask,
drowning your nightmares with a flask.

As the flawed you throw in the bin,
I look for the beauty within.
You are distracted by the Nines.
I seek baggage to go with mine.
As you converse so vapidly,
unaware of what I can see,
you laugh with disingenuous glee,
nescient to the man I can be.

So, swank away, and flip your hair,
stuffing your flaccid underwear.
Meanwhile, attentive, I'll listen.
But to me, it's rust that glistens.
I search for diamonds in the rough,
not pageantry, or hollow fluff.
While import you feign, I'll connect—
with the imperfectly perfect.

"COAHOMA, PART TWO"

Wintered winds wailed across forsaken plain,
as ceaseless snow and frost fiercely forayed,
unwaveringly, like blitheness's bane...

Daytimes passed to nights, evenings to twilight.
A Colorful coat of red dulled and greyed,
until time stuttered, stalled... then putrefied.

Seldom moonlit reprieves indeed did bring
requisite respite for frigid fatigue,
as snowy peaks subsided into Spring.

Though his mother's last plea flowed through his bones,
flames of fury seared, smoldered, then segued.
His once beating heart— to metamorphic stone.

As he traversed underneath starry skies,
yon rocky shore one moonless eventide,
he cursed the absent moon, with muddled eyes.

In darkened times of endless toil and strife,
where was his luminous, maternal guide?
Ire from cindered home twisted like a knife.

Orphaned, eld lost, he slept beneath heavens black...

CHAPTER SEVEN: TWILIGHT GRAY

"TAYO AY SAMA-SAMA (WE ARE TOGETHER)"

Yet another sunlit trail ends,
at the place where all stars must fall,
to return to their maker's hall,
beyond event horizon's bend,

Passed progressively failing hands...

Though thousands of twinkles I've seen
streak across night skies, then fade from view,
forgot, one dusk this would be you...
And though I know we'll meet in dream,

Each fallen star is a lost chance
not gleaming in your starstruck eyes...

For a thousand lifetimes, I've tried
to stop. To breathe. Move on. Believe...

But just can't leave all we conceived,
dreamt, upon that hidden hillside—

The twilit fans in foreign lands.
Butterfly smiles warming cold skies.
Two lonely souls shirking nightmares...

I think about you every time
I watch diamonds bring in the dawn,
and each sun rising over Bataan,
trailing from our loving pastime...

I recall, with each wondrous glance,
that fading stars don't really die—

Each night sky, a memory to share.

"THE EBB TIDE"

I stand upon a well-known pier,
gazing across the endless sea.
Unfettered bonds released from here,
umpteen dreams, possibilities,
yet only shades of you appear...

A breeze meanders over ebbing tide,
across unshaped landscapes hidden from view,
as adrift and defunct as inside,
retracing each explored avenue,
searching for even one trail untried...

Years uncounted like fleas in the sand,
gnawing and biting with wayward fret.
In mind and truth, every wonderland,
imagined scene lies just beyond, and yet...
the heart pines what the mind misunderstands...

Though starry eyes fill seas above, below,
each teeming with magic, promise and charm.
From parsecs of souls, was I whom you chose,
risking freedom, life, protecting from harm...
hence, whether shifting tides ebb, rise or flow...

I will forever be your rose.

"SANS MASQUE"

Sometimes, I feel...
I can't do this...
that I need someone,
whose actions match his words.
Whose heart at least speaks
the same language as mine.

Maybe I'm needy...
or maybe,
I just know what I need...
either way, at this point in life,
I can't settle for a reflection, or an echo.
Or a ghost.

I'm tired of sending messages
into the vacuum of cyberspace,
searching for nothing more
than the simple signs of life,
only to be met

with deafening silence...

Tired of sitting by the phone,
for hours and hours on end,
awaiting a call which never comes.
Tired of falling asleep
to the patter of my own tears...
Weary, am I... of goodbyes.

"FIELDS OF ASH"

Lying upon barren fields,
gazing up at ashen skies,
mulling over memories passed,
through seemingly endless nights...
Opposing poles misalign.
No teardrops remain to cry.
Sullen hues softly suffuse
fleeting coronal light...

Pungent clouds dissipate,
permeate stagnant spaces.
Stillborn, deflated dreams
resting upon unswept floors.
Pulses ebb, coagulate.
Idle eyes, vacant faces,
aimlessly pacing between
broken, decrepit doors...

Wherefore would scalding soirées
lead to lamenting lorn.
Notwithstanding fervent flames,
capricious storms, mourning morns.
Despite pursuits to placate dreads,
holding heads on broken hearts,
staved souls moored by thinning threads.
Lost in seas of riven parts...

Unfettered by hooking highs.
Entranced by elusive glows.
Shimmering sands 'neath moonlit skies,
where timeless tides freely flow...
E'en stars forget how to fly.
And grassy knolls have their lows,
but Bae must fight ‘til he dies.
From fields of ash, redwoods grow...

"SOULFUL EYES"

For Charlie

Apart in silence, we stand,
on the precipitous skirt,
betwixt the shades of eventide,
and rapture's vivid concert,
over familiar, distressed lands.

But in those bright, soulful eyes,
I see the enduring verve
of myriad stars alight,
ravishing dreams well-deserved,
each one a steadfast sunrise.

To dispel obscurity,
epiphanic truths impart,
and banish incessant night,
warming rigid, frigid heart,
absolving impurity.

Upon new exploits embarked,
when wandering starless skies,
remember the splendent light
within those keen, soulful eyes,
in times of unyielding dark.

CHAPTER EIGHT: MIDNIGHT BLACK

"ENTSCHULDIGUNG (SORROW)"

I float upon a wave.
Still. In silence.
Beyond time, and sight, and sense.
Rhythmically. Cyclically. Perpetually.
Concave.

I drift upon a sea.
Numb. Unseeing.
Without warmth, or light, or feeling.
Weightlessly. Breathlessly. Aimlessly.
Latchkey.

I glide upon a morrow.
Veiled. In pitch-black.
Devoid of hope, of life, of fallback.
I am sprawled. I am squalled. I am called.
Sorrow.

"ABADDON"

Fallen,
are your brethren of nine.
Each scored by blade, broken, line by line.
Tossed aside on crimsoned snow.
Cold. And dim. As candle's fleeting glow.
Forgotten.

Darkness
has fallen on this most unholy place,
plagued with festering disgrace.
Remains naught but hope abandoned,
once believed by your command, but
destroyed. Yet still.

Forlorn,
shrouded in darkness. Strength, mood, chance devoid,
fallen with broken knee, with sword still unemployed,
Felled,
by own most powerful weapon withheld.

Frozen,
with fear.

But you will not die here today!
Hearken without delay!
Take up your torch, sloughed mantle, and arise!
Let fill your veins, frenzied resolve of felled allies!
Donning shields of memories lived not in vain!
Steady your hand, armed with purpose unfeigned!

Live.
Hope.
Fight.
Liberate.
Love.
Teach.
Remember.

For those who once were.
For those who may never be.

.

"WAIT"

Countless epochs spent to compose,
budding dawn to setting sunlight—
an existence never meant to be...

Crucial factors, I once believed
to bring self-contented delight,
Produced in me fractures morose...

Winds of creation breathed my name.
Kismet's design led me to you.
Starry-eyed chimeras bore fools...

Yet, as twilight descends and cools,
and scarlet fades to midnight blue,
naught besides me remains to blame...

Gold hearts decayed to rusted tin,
upon crumbled castles of sand.
Crystalline drops coursed down my face...

We detached from our last embrace,
verklempt, incapable to stand,
as the despondent truth set in...

Beneath Stygian skies of glass,
on this unending, unlit night,
distantly, rings a musing strain,

A serendipitous refrain—
trust truth in one's own soulful light--
reminding that these woes will pass..."

Long after musing songs conclude,

And fade golden cycles of life,
beyond "insurmountable" strife,
lie untold days to start anew...

Be patient. Take courage. Have faith. Wait.

"TODAY, I DIED"

For the Lost, the Despaired and the Condemned

Today, I died.
No more hurt, or doubt, or fear.
No more worries, woes, or tears.
No more restless nights, watching them,
just breathing, through synthetic stems.
No more screaming at 3 a.m.,
at senseless fools to condemn.
Though I finally opened wide my eyes,
today, I died.

Today, I died.
No more stumbling, fumbling, bumbling at night.
No more cursing, fighting over who's right.
No more ear-busting shows during sleep hours,
or sleuthing whose hair keeps breaking showers.
No more nagging to turn off the bright lights.
Nothing but words left unsaid left to write;

I didn't really mind, I realized,
yet still, today, I died.

Today, I died,
so that tomorrow, I may rise again,
not in sorrow, anger, despair, or pain,
but with sense of hopeful purpose regained,
in unparalleled wonderment, unfeigned—-
a phoenix lily, sipping Spring's first rain,
peace, joy, compassion, coursing through my veins;
with love, and humble thanks in each reply--
but just for today, I may say... I died.

"CECIL'S PROVIDENCE"

For Alex

Darkened clouds billow from afar,
across mountaintops stained with blood,
air filled with scents of burning tar,
erasing memories of what's good...

Distant you look, disheveled hair.
Upon your face, despairing frown.
Behind you, all for which you care.
Onward, a journey yet unknown...

Loathe to tread this moonless night,
in your eyes, nothing left to cry,
accepting doom from endless plight,
as you release one final sigh...

Pushing upward off the ground,
you take a closing leap of faith.

In your heart, new hope you have found,
dispelling cackles from Hell's wraiths.

Skies alit with your resolve,
winds take up your sweetened scent.
Upon your breast, my healing salve.
Courageous, unwavering, unspent.

Now lost in snow as shadows rise,
I sing silently your lament—
lost dreams, fading from our eyes.
You fight for time the Fates have lent...

Their golden threads palely hang
from wayworn, forlorn, trembling hands.
Nearing knives, your waxing Yang,
toward unrelenting, desolate lands...

Memories of our sunny past,
filling your heart, mind, body, soul,
spreading above heavens so vast.
You soar en route to final goals...

Behind you, fleeting beams of light,
renewing within me our life,
as the present fades from sight.
Swiftly swings the golden knife!

Strings snap loudly, as times freeze,
this moment forever held in stance,
though star-crossed by a stagnant breeze.
Through timeless matrices we dance...

As memories begin to fade,
glowing embers, molten earth;
streaks of gold, unbroken jade,
from our ash, mercy's rebirth...

Though your tale may never be known,
lost amongst unending stars,
I still search for a holy knight,
where the calm quenches endless wars.

.

JOURNALS OF THE ERUDITE

CHAPTER NINE: DREAM VIOLET

"ALLEGORY OF THE FALLACIES OF MAN"

At the end of all things known and unseen,
in the wake of three ages concluded,
stood sons of Adam before squires divine,
to answer for fallacies colluded,
in the death of their mother, Saint Selene...

Across these ages, given boons pristine,
seven perversions these sons exuded,
soiling virtue with unholy designs,
inspiration with grandeur deluded,
charity with contempt for the gamine...

Rife with arrogance, anger, apathy,
avarice, ardency, antipathy,
appetite, were these sons, the squires opined,
and thus deserving of no sympathy
for havocs wrought by their psychopathy

By prideful malice were the meek enslaved,
made to suffer, starve by turned eyes and greed;
bodies broken by wrath and hate combined,
souls sold and rent by lustful gluttony;
their fields, houses and temples set ablaze.

These holy squires, numbered ten thousand, were
unanimous in verdict, penalty,
representing each faith thereto divined--
each son to be beaten, bound to a tree,
impaled by venomed blades, and massacred.

Afore each son's soul would then be unmade,
Adam's sons fell still, succumbed to despair,
accepting every charge as so assigned,
bereft of protest, resolve, even prayer,
that none more suffer by their hands depraved.

Ten thousand sacred swords rose overhead.
Yet stilling their blades-- three small, childlike hands,
victims of these sons, by cruelties devised.

Upon each scarred palm was a cattle's brand.
Upon each brow, ashen marks of the dead.

Although their names had long been forgotten,
each bore a grace, sealed by a solemn vow--
for innocence lost to schemes clandestine;
for futures pillaged by the here-and-now;
for blood spilled over spoils ill-begotten...

For mercy, the eldest prayed;
for hope, the middle implored;
for love, the youngest, in-kind...

That ones most helpless, pure of heart, should plea
a stay for the most wretched amongst men,
moved even the most stringent, resolved minds.
Shackles removed, each son went home again,
giving oath to atone, on bended knee--

Arrogance became Humility.
Avarice became Generosity.

Anger became Patience.
Antipathy became Kindness.
Ardency became Purity.
Appetite became Temperance.
Apathy became Diligence.

Thus, were fallacies of man, given chance,
Reborn by probity, not mere happenstance.

"WORLD'S EDGE"

At the world's edge, I search for you
where the misty meadows once grew.
Once resided the veins of life,
now poisoned with sorrow and strife

Unspoken words ring in my head,
echoing like wails from the dead.
In the canyons of dooming doubt,
forlorn, desolate, without clout.

Amongst the fog, your sunken face,
behind a mask of smiles and grace.
Uneasy, I stare in your eyes;
threnodies begin their reprise...

Abyssal heartache, I recall,
silently shuffling down the hall.
Anxiously impuissant, I gaze,
frozen in an eternal daze.

You make that catastrophic choice;
I cry with my taciturn voice.
Although it falls on deafened ears,
affirming my most grievous fears...

Pestilent bane defiles ichor.
Paralyzed, we lie on the floor,
as the moonlight in our eyes wanes,
and the lifeblood in our souls drains...

In the distance, a fading light
from an indiscernible height;
mystified, I begin to wake,
as my senses quiver and quake.

Listening to a far-flung whir,
futilely, you I try to stir,
fettered by melancholy mire,
With nothing for which to aspire...

Luminescence subdues and dims.
Frantically, I pull your limbs;
weeping, vital retreat draws nigh;
a heavy-hearted kiss goodbye.

"AT FIRST LIGHT"

Repose your frazzled head and mind.
Upon my shoulder to unwind
the ravels of this messy life,
and release your pain and strife.
The unending night is done;
at long last the war is won.
At first light, now you may rest,
As you sleep upon my breast...

A soothing sun slowly starts to rise
to dry your weary, grieving eyes.
Dream of hope's eternal reprieve,
and rainbows on dewy leaves.
Above, misty mountains wander;
no pestilent plights to ponder.
Let your angst subside;
no nighttime terrors to abide.

Hear the placid pulse of my heart.
Muse on divine dawn's serene start.
Let willful worries sink below,
as a balmy breeze softly blows.
You have arrived at journey's end,
where majestic marvels blend.
Feel tranquility steep your soul,
as you reach the ultimate goal.

May Somnus take you in arm,
Morpheus' wonders warm
the winter's unending frost
with bygone memories once lost.
Pietas on me now bestowed,
a parting kiss upon eyes closed.
Placing upon your crown, life's wreath.
Charon's obol, a closing breath.

"UWÄCHULEW'S REBIRTH"

On dry dunes of a once vast sea,
where untold marine fauna swam free,
and fertile lands bore giant trees,
remain naught but distant memories...

Amongst ruinous rubble and ash,
brought about by that fateful flash,
Pandora's Box the fools opened--
the beginning of the World's end...

Glorious glaciers thawed in plain sight;
sweltering sun, nefarious night,
as oligarchic greed fanned the flames,
while reenacting their Deadly Games...

Meanwhile, predicted plagues dispersed;
around the globe, soot and smoke cursed
Gaia's fate, as she withered and wept.
Beneath befouled Elysium she slept...

Frolicking forests forgotten;
copious crops, rancid and rotten--
War, Famine, Death ruled, unabated;
the Lifestream now desiccated...

The last tree cut, the last fish caught,
streams sullied, air arid and hot.
The indigent and wealthy clashed,
with nothing left to eat but cash.

The planet naught but ruined rock,
where the torpid pointlessly walked
in search of Valhalla, they sighed;
one by one, they toppled and died.

Where empires expired, they did land,
atop dismal desert and sand,
bygone generations did stand,
the Seed of Life in outstretched hands.

Forgotten Hope, they pulled from the box,
as they wound Father Time's busted clocks.
Life's Seed sewn, they prayed for Uwächulew's sake,
penitent for Man's fatal mistake.

As chagrined Chaac's tears began to rain
upon the dreary, desolate plain.
Uwächulew's aegis they did vow.
To guide their fate, descended the Crow

"MOONLIT MUSE"

A Pisces moon fills up the sky.
Indefinite egress draws nigh.
Sullen, speechless, one last embrace.
A feeble smile upon your face.
Twinkling tears descend from aloft,
like soothing rain, gentle and soft.
You pull away; the heart grows numb.
The crestfallen crystal succumbs,
silently shedding its last light...

Dimethyltryptamine cascades;
corporeal sentience fades.
repaid with the thousandth sweet kiss,
now awaited by Osiris.
As past, present and fate compress,
I reminisce, your voice, that dress;
rosé wine in a tiny bar,
all eyes on us, me on guitar,
silver moonlight shining so bright...

We must have conversed until dawn,
about dreams and hopes, come and gone.
My heart beating out of my chest,
you doted on my living zest.
When the whole had been told and said,
wine took hold; I slept on your bed...
You watched, softly humming our song,
as if nothing would ever go wrong,
stroking my hair throughout the night...

Though we must say our goodbyes,
before life's melody dies,
I'll remember, “carpe diem”—
your enduring words, priceless gems.
Faith in life and love, you renewed,
from the self-defeat I had brood.
Where meet battered shores, come find me,
in feathered streams of memory;
there, I'll await love's keen respite...

"PIECES OF ME"

Resting beneath a waxing, silver moon,
intertwined like cosmic DNA,
caressing skin with boundless tales portrayed,
nuzzled into your captivating grace,
sweetly, you dream to a soothing tune.

Two lonely hearts, gently pulsing pale light,
relearn a long-forgotten melody.
In a still-framed moment on Crossing Way,
without regard to time-- weightless, carefree--
even if only for a single night.

Though dreaming suns must rise, as days catch speed,
stay but one jif more, embraced in my arms,
under starry, sapphire skies by the Bay,
such that mind and heart keep you safe and warm.
Always true, like love's knot-- pieces of me.

"THE ETERNAL DREAMER"

Some see a cloud-skipping sun;
others, just a boy in the brume,
or remnant of a different brood.
I, a Middlemist Red in bloom,
whose beauty has just begun.

Though oft caught gazing at stars,
burning, as they fall from dark skies,
or absorbed in reflective moods,
watching his espied Geminis,
his dreams impart who we are—

Ramblers on forgotten shores;
hunters of our own piece of 'Home,'
tracking tanzanite violet-blue,
in fecund fields of mindful loam,
just seeking someone to hold.

Atop a utopic boon,
with ease, blinded by golden light,
looms still, the timeworn, bleeding yew--
slay no camellia with your blight;
leave be the boy with his moon.

CHAPTER TEN: INQUIRY RED

"PERCEPTIONS OF A MAN"

What is a man, in word and act?
Is he bold, enduring and strong,
uncontrolled by thought, will, or code,
never told, assuring no wrongs,
whether intended or in fact?

Who is a man, forwards and back?
High-powered, by rippling breakouts,
undeterred, never fraught at crossroads,
not cowered in crippling doubt,
no matter how his deck is stacked?

Why is a man, though, so kodak?
Never bleeding from broken heart,
nor conceding failed episodes,
never pleading for unspoken parts,
refusing to fall, or look back?

Doves.

Listen. Real men cry.
Some wear pink.
Men despair when brought to the brink.
Some even lip sync.
Others, shy.

Real men will mourn.
Some need helping hands.
Men falter, unkeen to e'en think.
Some have no homeland.
Wish to be unborn.

Real men cheerlead.
Some have worn a dress.
Men paint nails as well as they drink.
Some, feel lost; regressed... depressed.
Though, each deserves--and needs--

Love.

"FIFTY SUNS"

Once upon a half-century,
a young girl of renowned gentry,
unknowing of colors and shades,
wandered from her home in the glades.

From her haven of purest light,
glimpsed she glimmers of green and red,
beyond her world, benign and bright—
whereto great darkness had once spread.

Though, she, innocent and unlearned,
still not yet besieged by dark thralls,
meandered further from her walls,
entranced, mindless, unconcerned.

With each step, her light grew more faint,
as she pursued without constraint
the glisters just out of her reach,
'til, came she, upon pristine beach.

By her light, sands sparkled and shone,
like diamonds, circling black glass sea,
but as she crossed that shore unknown,
the sharp, knifelike beach made her bleed.

In stygian lake, deep she swam,
towards emerald, ruby bed,
until all her light had bled...
came ferryman, behest--two drachms

Devoid of mortal coil and coin,
offered she prized gems, yon adjoined.
"Fool girl," the ferryman disdained,
knowing well what dark soils contained.

Green-red treasures, her mind's eye glanced,
spurning true bounty for folly.
"Rage," was the blood-river expanse,
green beryl shore, he called, "Envy."

Lacking silver, ferryman quit.
Light-bereft, succumbed she to shade,
pining for her home in the glades.
Fifty suns-- lost-- in strayed orbit...

"HOW MANY TIMES?"

How many times, This One,
by door ajar, must you espy,
waiting like Hachikō-tan,
for his loved one, long demised?

With frostbitten, twilit grin,
dearest kin, say I to thee,
how many times, must parents pray,
for children long-lost at sea?

How many times, must gleaming suns
rise and fall, like empires of yore,
that they may warm far-flung faun,
yet not scorch even hither shores?

Through eras passed and those unseen,
even waning moons still condole,
with luminary empathy,
beacons for forlorn, wayward souls.

Whether in light or dark times,
despotic blight, or cordial climes,
burn bright, these pharos of Hope,
for we and they, who plea, pine, mope--

We mothers, fathers, kin, comrades-in-arms,
and lovers who wait, for that fateful day
chance returns to our doting arms, unharmed,
our special someones, loved ones, gone astray...

So, here, by casement ajar, I must endure,
flickering torch in unwavering hand--
night after night, age upon age, no detour--
unstitching, reweaving, each severed strand,

That his unbridled dole awake--
For as many times... as it takes.

"PERPLEXEDLY VEXED"

Pensive. Perplexed. Purportedly placated.
Obstacles obfuscate. Opalescence obliterated.
In innately intolerant instability,
which woeful, whispering wind
to tread, through thick and thin,
tenaciously?

Uninspired utility. Useless ubiquity.
Speciously suspended, sanctimoniously,
misrepresented, mischievously misconstrued.
Which way, when wailing wounding words,
feigning felicitous freedom, factual fords;
Infused? Imbued?

Dazed. Distracted. Doodling doddle.
Blenched beauty. Barren butane bottles.
Aspirations, arid atmospheres asphyxiate and ail.
Why would wooded worlds widen, when
elusive existential epiphanies ebb, expire, even?

Exhale.

Rouse. Ruminate. Revise rubric.
Leave. Lethal laments liquidate languid logic.
Sapphire sands solely surface surreptitiously. Surely.
When wishy-washy wacks waffle, wax,
vivify voracious violins. Vax.
Beam. Benevolently.

"WHY THE WIND BLOWS"

Often I return
to the place where the wind blows,
as I peer across
the barren land far below,
marred by drought and flame;
viewing past, future unfold
clouds of you roll by...

I won't teach, watch learn
the one I will never know—
about love and loss,
or nurture when you fail, grow,
guide through guilt or shame,
shoulder teardrops while I hold
back nightmares, dark skies...

Often my heart burns,
not knowing why the wind blows,
but seeing new moss

thrive again in stale hollows
reminds me don't blame
which way our written stones rolled,
for each sad goodbye

The wind may errantly blow—
a new chance my rose may grow.

"IGNES FATUI?"

Skin as smooth as mulberry silk,
spun from lulling clouds in flight.
Hair as lucent as autumn leaves,
catching the midmorning light,
as evanescing effluxion we bilk.

Eyes as clear as crystalline meres--
apt and boundless as cosmic skies.
Lips as soft and rare as vicuña fleece--
ethereal-- as timeless natural highs
extend from seconds, to days, to years...

Hearts rhythmically beating in sync,
like the sun, moon and passing stars.
Supple hands hold a warming face,
twain souls embraced in ardent arms,
bonded by adamantine links.

A zephyr sustains fervent flames.
Symbiotic in unity,
enamored fingers interlace,
entwined in perpetuity--
moments suspended in still frames.

"DUAL DUELS"

On this day,
sitting upon ledge,
two contrasting horizons--
seamless, without edge;
unassayed.

On this day,
above, endless skies--
weightlessly free, not wizened;
below, seas of ties--
faraway.

On this day,
of woes well-aware,
tolls unpaid, sacrificed suns,
sharing without spare;
disarrayed.

Each step we climb,
to better clime;
each steep ascent,
battered assent,

Brings us back to this slump...

On this night,
beyond brood or care,
watching cars in lapsing time,
as each pays its fare--
Red, gold, white.

On this night,
beneath twinkling stars--
seas as soothing as sublime--
Celestial memoirs,
Writs of light.

On this night,
melodic bubbles

meander beyond couth rhyme,
passed the Great Hubble,
Out of sight.

Each moon which mourns
the rising morns,
each son's descent--
raising dissent--

Effects a hurdling hump...

Though, hurdles and humps
were meant to be jumped.

CHAPTER ELEVEN: DISCOVERY ORANGE

"ANGST IN YOUR EYES"

I can see the angst in your eyes;
definitely been there before...
desecrated dreams, savage lies
broken-hearted, crushed at the core

In such an uncertain place,
where everything's turned upside-down,
hard to know which path, which face,
or even which way the wind's blown

As I look upon your fading smile
not seen the sunlight in a while,
know you are never, ever alone...

So, take my gentle, outstretched hand;
make that first step in this unplanned
happenstance adventure we've grown.

Can't promise butterflies or rainbows,
not glitz, glam, glitter or gold;
life, love, happiness, ebb and flow,
rather-- warmth, in the bitter cold

The little I have on this rocky earth,
I will share, even give to you;
though, from within, comes true mirth--
making memories, old and new.

"PORES AT EARLY DAWN"

Quietly perched upon a cashmere cloud,
I gaze across the sleepy vista view,
watching everything-- and nothing at all;
alone, with my musings of I and you--
A packed room; chance embrace; enchanting crowd...

Colorful candy, aquamarine hair;
house on a hill, and plush valentine cub;
a small, playground swing... the ensuing Squall.
Two protostars, scions of peace and love,
but too green for honest truths to lay bare...

But, its own master, is an ebullient dream,
full of diamond skies, and rosy moonlight.
And yet, I keep going back to that hall--
the warmth of your arms; snugly swaddling, tight—
oxytocin, perhaps; so real it seemed...

Rhapsodical rumination followed,
being referred to for the foremost time.
Someone's paramour, there, braced by that wall.
Our first kiss-- though impalpably sublime,
it left hurt, envy, spite, in that hollow...

As I peer down this steep mountain of mine,
dawn's first light begins to brush the shipyard.
Those three words, I yearned so long, I recall,
and yet, here we are, with bygone postcards,
as paths cross once more, and stars realign,

But before any entranced dance begins,
just promise me that whatever may come,
growingly climb, glowingly rise— or fall—
speak true. Be you, and you've already won.
Though a demure murre, headfirst I'll dive in.

"MI CORAZÓN, BAE"

You are the sun,
enduring and bright.
I am the moon,
filled with your light.

When you are away,
my emotions rage, and sway.
But each time when I break,
you hold me while I'm weak,

So I can reset, through sleep,
returning, once more, to me.
This is why I hold on
to our broken memories.

"DAVID"

Many lifetimes ago,
when the sun first began to rise—
before the seven seas swelled, raged and froze—
before bubbles filled and capsized—
was David on Van Gough.

Sye, a kid of nineteen,
swimming freestyle in a deep pool,
met with David at The Withering Rose,
a haven for kings, swain and fools,
over scones and caffeine.

Though not terribly aged,
of uncharted, moonlit star-cross
David spoke, in both poetry and prose—
enchanting tales of love, and loss,
as he took center stage.

While they talked through the night,
sharing words each had never heard,
amongst the boulevards of broken homes,
the lines of dreams and passions blurred,
as they bathed in firelight.

On a bridge for lost souls,
Sye engaged in real love's first kiss--
as sweetly apt as honeyed palindromes,
floating on a cloud of remiss,
soon to smash into shoals.

Commingling until daybreak,
David dreamed, Sye upon his heart,
dreading his return to the 'catacombs'—
the world that would keep them apart,
once they were forced to wake.

Thus, for those fleeting hours,
onto David, Sye tightly held,
his scent like fresh blossoms on a Spring breeze.

But when at last their time was felled,
Sye left those sweet flowers...

Twenty years in rear view,
after strings of unopened mail,
failed romances, broken vows, returned keys,
Sye mulled in emotional gaol,
over chances eschewed.

In a forgotten box,
a letter marked two thousand three
still smelled of hydrangeas of the Northeast,
from times carefree, naivety,
penned by teary flummox.

It spoke of love not decreed--
restless eves, mused on failure's truth;
wishes to share a long goodbye one day,
upon the lost bridge of their youth...
signed, “Lovingly, Your David.”

One night, frozen in time,
undimmed by even two hundred moons,
burned bright in Sye, who left without delay
to the place their hearts first attuned,
beyond reason or rhyme.

But when Sye found The Rose,
in its place, vacant ruins stood...
Sye wept for hours, ‘til Sye’s warm hands he embraced.
Beyond era or age, they would
love, be loved, he proposed--

Sye's David on Van Gough.

"LOCUS CONCURSUS"

In distant, bygone memory,
seemingly not so long ago,
when hope and dream convened,
without affray or much ado,
illusion and reality...

In that place, where was undiscerned
will from wish, deed from feted awe,
triune founders, in still-framed scene--
Visioned Maker; Forger of Law;
Maternal Phare-- warm gaze downturned...

In that moment, immune from time,
miracles wrought from mere notion;
swords of justice, astute and keen;
lucent compass; quelled black ocean;
guiding home souls lost to foul climes,

Gifting shield, cloth, undue reprieve,
with unabated, loving mercy.

"LIVE AND LOVE"

'You gaze at me, with piercing eyes,
asking questions about my demise.
Where have you been these twenty years,
bringing light to my buried fears;
offering faulty remedies,
for desolation no one sees.
My barren heart has no key.
If you really care, let me be...

'What you want, kid? Why you still here?
I will be abundantly clear--
you come from a world with blue skies,
not torment, screams or endless lies.
Long ago, we might have been friends,
but some events, time never mends.
Save your effulgence from above
We are both not ready for love.'

Pain and sorrow may endure,
defiling everything pure;
shadows may lurk all around,
stifling each and every sound.

Fear of hurt, hiding in the dark,
where trauma ails, poignant and stark;
though suffering what life has thrown,
know, that you are not alone.

No solutions, or easy fix
for tall walls made of bloodied bricks;
still, need not silently suffer,
behind a hardened heart's buffer.

Untold pain eases, and ebbs,
for those who fight despondent webs.
'Not ready for love,' possibly...
but you're still worthy to be free.

Let luminance fill your heart,
to repair what fell apart.
So petrifying, I know,
to let the lifestream freely flow...

Journeys start with a single step;
let courage rise where darkness slept.
Take my hand, let go of the past;
dwell not in fear-- live; love, at last.

"(UN)BROKEN"

No matter how thin, not slim enough.
No matter how apt, not up to snuff.
Despite what I draw, write or sing,
or how much good cheer I (can) bring,
always a reason to rebuff.

Even how much saved, too much spent.
Each fear braved, I'm too broken, bent.
For each stone placed upon my crown,
each meter I swim, and don't drown--
just another feat to be rent.

Reflecting on Crater Lake's face,
wondering wherein lies my place,
showers of stars fall from sullen skies.
Epiphanies materialize--
your own defeats were the disgrace.

From festering pools of regret,
and fizzled dreams you can't forget,
you have to eclipse blazing suns,
unaware you're the toxic one;
you create snags where none exist...

Today,
I rive that fettered net.

Sirius has awoken,
with lucent, glaring token.
No longer shall I lie numb,
stoical, passive or dumb.

Today,
I choose to be unbroken.

CHAPTER TWELVE: SAGACIOUS CYAN

"DO IT FOR YOU"

When summertime friends thin and fade,
as sleet starts to fall from dark skies--
when you've lost with every card played,
and left with mountains of goodbyes--
Do it for you...

When you feel no one 'really' cares,
or nothing matters in the end--
when you figure no point is there,
for your rent scars and wounds to mend--
Do it for you...

When you try and fail, fall and cry,
seek the holy grail, fight for blithe trails--
when you're bled till frail, left for dead,
and end up alone on an unused shelf--
Do it for you.

Toss every notion and hateful lie,
every stigmatized blossom you've dried,
from those who made you feel unworthy--
Get up. Show up. Be your own beauty.
Do it for you.

Whether with unkempt, wind-blown hair,
or highly misunderstood flair--
with broken masks, or empty flasks--
even old change, though defunct, strange,
To someone has value... (you...)

So. Do it. For you.

"WEEP NOT"

Weep not for the departed,
fallen, or those who have passed--
their voyage begins anew;
let the salty, sullen drops,
the warmth of memory's hearth,
be sorrow's panacea,
as the flames of rebirth rise,
and cinders climb the night sky...

Instead, grieve for those who live--
the destitute, and forlorn--
those who struggle to endure;
let brokenhearted ashes
be empathetic embers,
to feed faint, famished fires,
and soften frostbitten souls--
be they kin, estranged, unknown...

Uplift life's luminescence,
so compassionately drawn
from universal union;
see the strife of weary woes,
worn by fraying, frazzled shoes,
traversing tearful, trodden trails;
be a benevolent beacon--
for the lost, in troubled times.

"PEACE"

Peace is the morning light,
gently rising over the darkness,
over crests of hilltop fields, in silhouette,
abound with the soft glow
of orange-red daylillies...

Peace is the familiar hymn,
borne warmly of a mild breeze,
permeating the cold, foggy mist,
climbing down majestic mountain peaks,
serendipitously sprinkled with snow...

Peace is the dewdrop at dawn,
left by tumultuous, overnight storms,
wrested perfectly, in loving palm fronds
nurturing, offering needed respite,
to battered travelers below...

Peace is the adoring mother,
fingers running tenderly through silken hair
of her un-aging, resting child--
lashes still dusted with dashes of starlit fantasy--
halcyon days upon their hearts...

Peace is the Mighty Ash,
courageously rising from dark soil,
stretching long fingertips heavensward.
No woe or sorrow may obscure
its fervent pursuit of a dream—

For brighter skies;
of temperate climes;
to one day hold upon breast
sunlit child of its own.

Patienter vive. Vive in amore.
Esto benignus. Et in pace.
In Patience, live. Live, in love.
Be Kind. And in Peace.

"HONORABLE"

Honorable is not one in search of glory,
or riches, power, awards or fame,
whether for country, lord or private quarry.

Virtuous, rather, are they who labor each hour,
to soothe the weary, woeful and unnamed,
be it nosh, salve, tissue or sunflower.

Just is not vengeance or karmic plea,
more so unbidden quarter, and gruntled candor;
prudence in evinced compassion, courage, charity.

Wise isn't he fore lectern, soapbox or common stream.
Sage is the humble, honest, inconspicuous creek,
whose sacrificed tributes fill lakes, oceans, dreams.

More puissant is patient pen than strong-armed blade,
inkwells stocked by jerkwater journeys amidst the meek
by lone lessons learned, and forlorn farewells bade.

Breathe, then, for brothers, sisters, child or neighbor,
and the despondent strangers on foreign shore—
live, therefore, in honor.

"LIGHT"

I am light.
Warm, sun-kissed rays, peeking betwixt trees,
over snowy mounts on Spring's first breeze,
across poppied plains, in vibrant valleys;
welcomed repose from Heimal freeze...

I am the wind.
Ancient whispers, rolling off pines,
singing amongst fenny reeds,
sweeping passed sandy cacti spines,
en route to where rivers meet seas...

I am the earth.
Fortuitous fruitions
of chaos, calamity, and calm;
solid stone, crafted through eons--
robust, resolute, resilient...

I am shadow.
A misunderstood mystery,
absent which, no star could aptly shine,
nor weary vagabond find ease
from waxing sol on his cumbrous climb...

I am water.
Heavenly drops, dispersed beyond realms,
from alpine lakes, to falls unfound,
quenching arid sands overwhelmed;
life, respite, soothing seaside sound...

I, too, am fire.
Persistent passion, burning bright.
Radiant warmth, fervent drive,
in sleet, snow, on dark, lonesome nights,
to revive, stay alive, and thrive...

I am lightning.
Quick to act, adapt and change.
Unpredictable, and untamed.

Destructive at far or close range,
empowered, when aptly contained...

I am the frost.
Collected, and cool in mind, soul;
unwavering, in law and rule.
Purposefully focused on goal;
impartially stern to fools...

As I learn, grow, and elate,
with each hue of humanity,
I find peace and love amongst hate;
each color, shade created me.
For, I.. am light.

"COAHOMA, PART THREE"

Upon a chilled, remote and sandy strand,
there lay a smothered, slumbering son,
astray in a hereto uncharted land.

Eftsoon untold enduring, starless nights,
arose the tender, dawning glow of sun,
springtime respite from windy, brumal bites.

Auspicious as a maternal caress,
across the scarred fell of her fallen cub,
her sole progeny's crown upon her breast.

From the obscured depths of Oneiric cores,
softly quavered an empathetic dub,
whose humble tune reached even lucid moors--

A dirge, for bygone lives, kin; forfeit love,
lovelorn hearts, blighted by unyielding loss,
dreams rent asunder, on fractured floors above...

Avulsions begot by misguided trust,
wilted daisies on desiccated moss;
dazzling diamonds ground into rusted dust...

But budding sprouts may grow, from doleful tears;
graphene shields, made from mirthful memories,
to mend shattered souls, by assuaging fears...

Awoke, then he, with sanguine will resown;
deeply, he understood these threnodies--
For, none is ever, truthfully, alone...

And he followed trails back to his homeland.

"THE REST OF FOREVER"

For Charles, in the Best Love Story Ever Told

As we lie beneath a full moon,
with grins as wide as it is blue,
thinking how far we've come since you
brought me into your world last June,

With just a hand, and your sweet smile,
rearranging my frenzied hair,
you broke my walls, lay my heart bare,
showing me just how worthwhile

Is this great love story of ours,
beneath a cozy coat of stars...

Can't help but get lost in the glow,
eyes reflecting your soul's pure light--
gentle and wise, both true and bright--
mending wounds from so long ago.

It was just us against remorse,
drifting somewhere in stellar seas;
Through it all, you stayed here with me,
when stormy winds blew us off course.

As my lips draw closer to yours,
I'm thankful for these timeless hours...

I would search ten thousand lightyears--
knowing deep in this beating heart
you taught to love when we're apart--
to once again, be with you here,

Sharing this love, untouched by time,
atop these vast mountains we climbed--
bodies, minds, and souls intertwined,
beyond cold reason, spectral rime--

Spending the rest of forever,
In the best love story... Ever.

"FORGIVENESS"

Forgiveness
is a subtle word,
in an unending sea
of colloquially
repressed memory.

Frequently misused,
cast into the clouds,
often abused,
with thunderous clout,
excessively.

Made into a crutch,
shaped like divine touch,
to try to bury
the raging fury,
and upheaval.

We scuttle unheard,
‘cause this simple word–
seems inept,
incomplete,
insufficient,
incompre-
-hensible.

So then.
What does it mean?
To truly forgive?

Forgiveness
is a warm home to come
for the brother who shunned
you so very long ago…

Forgiveness
is a long hug for ones
who ripped rugs from their sons’
feet, learning still to grow…

Forgiveness
is the cold morning dew–
for those many of you,
whose great burdens and pains
made straight guerdons of veins–

To cool, soothe and heal
fiery hatred you feel
for yourself and the four
who took turns pricking holes
in your mind, heart and soul,
as you 'rightly' writhed and squealed,
watching you bleed on the floor…

Forgiveness
is looking in their eyes,
with genuine goodwill,
despite
the parts you sacrificed,
while trying hard to stay chill,
and not be defined— each night—

by the unyielding hurt,
rightful wrath they deserved,
for battering you,
shattering you,
DEEP
throughout your core…

Forgiveness
will let go of the past
to find forgotten paths,
away from stained bloodbaths…

Forgiveness
is knowing our lost futures
aren't defined by frayed sutures,
but by peace, and calm, that last–
floating,
on the feathers,
of Forgiveness.

"CHEROKEE BLESSING"

May the warm winds of Heaven blow softly on your home, and the Great Spirit bless all who enter there.

May your moccasins make happy tracks in many snows, and each rainbow always touch your shoulder.

Acknowledgements

Special thanks to all the people who inspired, encouraged, promoted and believed in me, including but not limited to my husband, my friends, family, my second-year college English teacher, and of course, you the readers. Without all of you, I may never have put words to paper.

So, thank you. From the bottom of my heart.

www.ingramcontent.com/pod-product-compliance
Lightning Source LLC
LaVergne TN
LVHW041811060526
838201LV00046B/1222